Charles Mackay

New Light on some Obscure Words and Phrases in the

Works of Shakespeare and his Contemporaries

Charles Mackay

New Light on some Obscure Words and Phrases in the Works of Shakespeare and his Contemporaries

ISBN/EAN: 9783337253493

Printed in Europe, USA, Canada, Australia, Japan

Cover: Foto ©Thomas Meinert / pixelio.de

More available books at **www.hansebooks.com**

NEW LIGHT

ON

SOME OBSCURE WORDS AND PHRASES IN THE WORKS OF SHAKSPEARE AND HIS CONTEMPORARIES.

BY

CHARLES MACKAY, LL.D.

AUTHOR OF "THE GAELIC (ANCIENT BRITISH) ETYMOLOGY OF THE LANGUAGES OF WESTERN EUROPE, AND MORE ESPECIALLY OF THE ENGLISH AND LOWLAND SCOTCH."

London :

REEVES & TURNER, 196, STRAND, W.C

1884.

H.R.H. THE PRINCE LEOPOLD (DUKE OF ALBANY).
THE DUKE OF DEVONSHIRE.
THE MARQUIS OF HARTINGTON.
THE EARL OF DERBY.
THE EARL OF SOUTHESK.
LORD WOLVERTON.
THE BARONESS BURDETT COUTTS (2 *Copies*).
LORD WAVENEY.
LORD REAY (2 *Copies*).
LORD TENNYSON.
SIR JOHN LUBBOCK, Bart., M.P.
SIR ARTHUR J. OTWAY, Bart., M.P.
SIR ERASMUS WILSON, F.R.S.
SIR JAMES CAIRD, K.C.B.
HENRY IRVING, Esq.
JOHN PAYNE COLLIER, F.S.A. (*deceased*).
SIR JOHN GILBERT, R.A. (2 *Copies*).
ALFRED MORRISON, Esq. (6 *Copies*).
B. LEIGH SMITH, Esq. (5 *Copies*).
WM. HAZLITT, Esq. (Registrar in Bankruptcy).
SIR THEODORE MARTIN (2 *Copies*).
JOHN WALTER, Esq., M.P.
S. MORLEY, Esq., M.P.
J. O. HALLIWELL-PHILLIPS, Esq.
P. H. MUNTZ, Esq., M.P.
JUSTIN McCARTHY, Esq., M.P.
SAMUEL TIMMINS, Esq., F.S.A. (Birmingham).
J. PYM YEATMAN, Esq.
COLIN RAE BROWN, Esq.
HENRY RUSSELL, Esq.
MRS. MOUNSEY BARTHOLOMEW.

Dr Campbell Morfit.

Miss Morfit

Bernard Quaritch, Esq.

Charles H. Russell, Esq.

Conde de Casa Gonzalez.

George Hawkes, Esq.

Wm. Black, Esq.

James Smith, Esq. (Glasgow).

George Urf, Esq. (Glasgow).

The Mitchell Library (Glasgow).

P. Comyn Macgregor, Esq. (Paisley)

Charles de la Prymt, Esq.

Dr. Tanner.

C. E. Flower, Esq., Stratford-upon-Avon.

Messrs. Trubner & Co. (4 *Copies*).

Public Library, Boston, Massachusetts.

Alfred Russell Smith (2 *Copies*).

S. C. Hall, Esq., F.S.A.

J. C. Magrath, Esq.

G. W. Nicholls, Esq. (Glamorgan).

G. W. Petter, Esq. (Messrs. Cassell & Co.).

Adam Holden, Esq. (Liverpool).

Messrs. Blackwood & Co. Edinburgh (2 *Copies*).

James B. Brown, Esq. (Selkirk).

James Ral, Esq.

Reform Club Library.

Archibald Hood, Esq. (Cardiff).

Cluny Macpherson, of Cluny, Esq.

A. L. Elder, Esq.

John Mackay, Esq. (Swansea).

John Mackay, Esq. (Ben Reay).

Edwin Arnold, Esq.

George Routledge, Esq.

Robert Hepburn, Esq.

Lachlan Mackinnon, Esq. (Skye).

James Hedderwick, Esq. LL.D. (Glasgow).

Rev. James Stormonth (*deceased*).

T. L. Oxley, Esq. (*deceased*).

Subscribers' Names, already received.

W. W. TUCKER (Boston, Massachusetts).
F. DE M. LEATHES, Esq.
G. MAUDE ALLEN, Esq.
G. J. GRAY, Esq.
THE REV. ALDIS WRIGHT (Cambridge).
RICHARD GIBBS, Esq.
A. L. ELDER, Esq.
A. VIGORS O' DWYER, Esq.
J. T. MAYBANK, Esq. (Dorking).
Mrs. ROBERT REECE.
Miss BERTHA DE VYVER.

Subscribers' Names will be received by the Author, Fern Dell, Dorking; and by Messrs. Reeves & Turner, 196, Strand, London, W.C.

PREFACE.

꙳ᮂᮂᮂ꙳

ALL students and lovers of Shakspeare are aware that there are many obscure and unintelligible words and phrases in his Plays and Poems, as well as in those of his most eminent contemporaries, which his editors and commentators have hitherto been unable to explain. Critical examination proves that a large proportion of these are traceable to the Keltic, Gaelic, or Gallic spoken by the Britons who possessed the country before the irruption of the Danes and Saxons, or the formation of the actual English language. This ancient, but long unwritten speech, though Dr. Samuel Johnson and others, who spoke without knowledge, were of a contrary opinion, was not wholly superseded by the Anglo-Saxon, but remained to a very considerable extent in use among the labouring classes and the unliterary population, until long after the time of Shakspeare, and exists to the present day in many slang and unliterary words and the colloquial lanquage of the uneducated or semi-educated vulgar. By the lights derived from these hitherto-neglected sources, the Author has been enabled to explain many passages in these immortal works, which have been puzzles and stumbling-blocks to English scholars for nearly three centuries.

The work, of which the following pages are offered as a specimen, appeals to all admirers of the poet, and to such students of philology as are ready to receive the truth whencesoever it may come, and however much it may run counter to the preconceived opinion that the English language is wholly of Saxon or Anglo-Saxon derivation ; and that it is in no way indebted to the original speech of the British people.

8

The Edition—handsomely printed on fine paper, small quarto ... be strictly limited to *Two Hundred and Fifty Copies*, each ... will be numbered and certified by the signature of the ... and of which the price to the origina' subscribers will be One Guinea, and to non-subscribers One Guinea and a-Half.

INTRODUCTION.

-~෴~-

THERE are many words and phrases in the works of
Shakspeare, and in those of the poets and dramatists of the
Elizabethan era that are obsolete or unintelligible, or have
changed their primitive meaning. Some of the obscurities
that have long puzzled commentators are evident errors of
the press, for Shakspeare seems never to have corrected his
proof-sheets, like the authors of our time, and was so sin-
gularly careless of his literary fame, except in the instance
of his early and very beautiful poems, *Venus and Adonis*
and the *Rape of Lucrece*, as to allow printers and publishers
to attribute to him many works, unworthy of his reputa-
tion, which he never wrote, and to publish his undoubted
works without his sanction. This circumstance accounts
for many errors that have crept into the text, but leaves
unexplained a great number of words that must have been
current in his time, or he would not have used them, but
which dropped out of literary fashion in the courtly and
corrupt time of Charles II., and in that of Dryden and Pope
when classicism all but killed romanticism in the current
literature of the upper classes.

It is very clear that Shakspeare did not derive all his
words from the dictionaries, but that he made a free use of
the vernacular and unliterary speech of the people of his
time and of the midland districts of England, to which
London did not wholly give the literary law, as it did a

century later The dictionaries of his time were few and
of small value, and not one of them recognized the fact
that the English language was not wholly drawn from
the Flemish, the French, or the Latin. No account was
made of the Keltic element in the common speech of
the labouring classes. It was generally and implicitly
believed that the early inhabitants of Britain who spoke
Keltic, though spared by the Romans during nearly
five centuries of occupation, were exterminated after the
Romans left by the Saxons and Danes, with the excep-
tion of a few who fled to Normandy and Brittany or
took refuge in Wales and Cornwall, or fled across the Clyde
to the mountains of Scotland. This erroneous idea, that
rested solely upon the authority of Gildas, possibly a good
monk, but certainly an untrustworthy historian, prevailed
until Dr. Johnson compiled his pretentious and often erroneous Dictionary in the eighteenth century, and has more
or less coloured every dictionary that has been subsequently
published. It is beginning, however, to be understood that
though many thousands, it may be hundreds of thousands,
of the Britons were slain, and dispossessed of their lands,
and reduced to feudal servitude by the Danes and the
Saxons, they were not exterminated ; that their extermina-
tion was not so much as attempted or advocated ; that the
invaders who came to the country without women inter-
married with the British, and that the ancient language of
the mothers of the new and mixed race remained partially
existent in the new generation. It was this British or
Gaelic, and partially Kymric, element of the language,
scarcely understood and wholly despised by the governing
classes, that in after years became known as " slang " or
" cant," all the words of which were declared by Johnson
and his equally ignorant predecessors and successors to be

"without etymology." But, as has been said in our day by
the Duke of Somerset, "every word in every language has
its pedigree." There is not a slang or cant word in English
—or in any of the languages of Europe—that has not its
etymology as clearly traceable as the more classic words
that have been admitted to the honours of literature. Mid-
England, where Shakspeare was born and bred, was not so
thoroughly Saxonized, either in speech or blood, as the
southern and eastern shores of the island. The forest of
Arden, where he chased the deer, means in Keltic the
"high" forest. His mother's name was Keltic, if not
his father's; for it is possible that Shakspeare is but a
Saxonized corruption of the Keltic Schaespeir, or Chaksper,
as his father's name was written, which signifies,—*shac* or
seac, dry, and *speir* shank; as we have in our day the
Saxon names of Sheepshank and Cruikshank, suggested
by a personal malformation or deformity in days when
surnames were not common, and applied as a nickname
to some early ancestor of the family. Not alone Shakspeare, but Spencer, Ben Jonson, Marlow, Massinger, Beau-
mont and Fletcher, and other writers of that time, employed
British words, which were then well understood, but which
have not been explained by modern commentators, for the
sufficient reason that they have never looked for the explanations in the only place where it is possible to find
them—the language of the Saxon and Flemish Britons,
and of the sons of British mothers, who retained in after-
life the homely words of the nursery and the workshop.
And the very name of Anglo-Saxon—long erroneously
supposed to be compounded of Angle in Jutland, and
Saxon from the German principality of Saxony—unknown
in that early day,—is a proof of the fusion of the British
with the Germanic race. *Angle* is in all probability but a

Teutonic corruption of the Keltic *In-gael* - "the Gael" or
Kelts—so that the very name of England—or *Angle*-land
is the land of the Gael, and not the land of the Teutons
or Saxons.   Scholars who have taken the pains to investi-
gate the truth of traditionary opinions and derivations, and
who have been, moreover, led astray by the erroneous history of Gildas, and his successors who accepted his state-
ments without inquiry, all agreed to ignore the British
element in the language, or to confine it to Wales, Cornwall,
the Highlands of Scotland, and portions of Ireland.   But
the language never wholly died out of England proper,
though it was to a large extent superseded by the use,
among the literary and educated classes, first of the so-
called Saxon or Teutonic substratum brought in by the
invaders, and by the second French stratum, itself of Keltic
origin, superadded by the Normans.

That the Keltic and Gallic, or Gaelic, language was at
one period spoken all over the West and South of Europe
is evident from the fact that all the great rivers and mountains in those ranges of the Continent derived their names
from the Gauls : or the primitive people who spoke Gallic,
or Gaelic, and who, swarming out of Asia, first overran and
colonized Greece, Italy, Spain, France, a part of Germany,
and the whole of the British Islands.   There were two
branches of the Keltic people : first the Gauls, who spoke
the Keltic, Gallic, or Gaelic, language still living, though
with impaired and perishing vitality, in the Highlands of
Scotland and the West of Ireland ; second, the Kymri,
whose language is yet vigorous in Wales and in Brittany,
and which has but lately and within living memory died out
of Cornwall.   The Kymric branch of the Keltic has been
thought by many scholars, who were ignorant of the Gallic,
or Gaelic, branch, to have named the rivers of Europe ; but

that this is an error will become evident to every scholar who, without the prejudice of preconception, will conscientiously endeavour to trace such names as the Danube, the Rhine, the Rhone, the Thames, the Severn, and the countless Avons in England, Scotland, and Ireland, to their original language; and such names of mountain ranges as the Ural, the Alps, the Appennines, the Carpathians, and the Pyrenees to their roots. These are invariably Gallic, and not Kymric.

"It cannot be doubted," says the late eminent "Anglo-Saxon scholar," Mr. J. M. Kemble, in the preface to the third volume of his *Codex Diplomaticus Ævi Saxonici*, published by the English Historical Society, "that local names, and those devoted to distinguish the natural features of a country, possess an inherent vitality which even the urgency of conquest is frequently unable to destroy. A race is rarely so entirely removed as not to form an integral, though subordinate, part of the new State based upon its ruins ; and in the case where the cultivator continues to be occupied with the soil, a change of master will not necessarily lead to the abandonment of the names by which the land itself, and the instruments or processes of labour, are designated. On the contrary, the conquering race are apt to adopt these names from the conquered ; and thus, after the lapse of twelve centuries and innumerable civil convulsions, the principal words of the class described·yet prevail in the language of our (the English) people, and partially in our literature. Many, then, of the words which we seek in vain in the 'Anglo-Saxon' dictionaries are, in fact, to be sought in those of the Kymri,—from whose practice they were adopted by the victorious Saxons in all parts of the country. They are not 'Anglo-Saxon,' but Welsh, very frequently unmodified either in meaning or pronunciation."

The argument in this passage is irrefutable—the only

error of Mr. Kemble being that he attributes to the Kymric that which belongs to the Gallic, or Gaelic, branch of the Keltic language : an error of which the accomplished writer himself would have been convinced, if he had endeavoured to trace any of the names of the mountains and rivers of the European continent to the language of Wales. The Kymri, it is true, have *dur* and *afon* for river, as the Gael have *dur* and *abhuin*. These words enter into the name of many European rivers, as the *Douro* in Portugal, the *Dur*ance in France, and Aber*dour*, the confluence of the *Dur* with the Firth of Forth, in Fifeshire. The Kymric and the Gaelic *abhuin* (Avuin give names to the countless Avons (beginning with Shakspeare's Avon, Stratford-upon-Avon) that are to be found in England, Scotland, and Ireland, as well as to the "havens" in every part of the Coast; but such names as the Usk, the Esk, the Ouse, the Ose, the Isis—which are all traceable to the Gallic or Gaelic *uisque* (water), but not to the Welsh or Kymric. The Kymri undoubtedly gave names to the most prominent natural objects and features of the scenery in Wales and Cornwall, a portion of the South-West of England, and of the opposite coast of Brittany; but the Kymric was confined to one corner of Europe and of England, and, unlike the Gallic, or Gaelic, was not spoken in Gaul, Italy, Spain, and the greater portion of the British Isles. It was mainly the Gallic, or Gaelic, element, and in a smaller degree the Kymric, that remained in England to permeate the speech introduced by the invading Danes and Saxons, and which, in intimate, though unrecognised, union with the Teutonic, formed the *Anglo-Saxon*, and afterwards the English language as it was spoken, though not always written, in the age of Shakspeare. English Lexicographers, buiding solely on the Saxon foundation, ignored the previous and not annihilated language of the British or Keltic people, and allowed prejudice to stand in lieu of investigation. "The weak point in all the learned," says the Introduction to "Spoon and Sparrow," by the Rev. Oswald Cockayne, "is their ignorance. The laity do not assume to know anything; yet in an Englishman's mother tongue, few clowns but could puzzle a doctor." It was this which puzzled the learned Dr. Johnson, and which has puzzled his successors in the industry of compiling Dictionaries, from the days of that ponderous pundit to our own. All these laborious followers in a beaten track have agreed to ignore the language of their British ancestors, and have sought everywhere for the origin of obscure English words, except in the fountain-head.

"I," says Nares in the Preface to his valuable Glossary, "have particularly avoided deriving common English words from languages of which the people who employed them must have been entirely ignorant : a method which some etymologists have pursued to a very ridiculous extent." But Nares did not rigorously practise what he preached, and looked to every imaginable source for the explanation of an obsolete or archaic English word, rather than to the English of the common or unlearned English people, who had Keltic blood in their veins and Keltic words on their tongues. It is my object to prove, from Shakspeare and the writers of his time, that this Gaelic, or Keltic, element formed a considerable portion of the vernacular speech of that day, as it does of this, and to illumine by this new light many of the obscure words and passages in the great poet's works, which none of his editors and commentators (all of whom have been ignorant of Kymric and Gaelic) have hitherto been able to explain.

CHARLES MACKAY.

Keltic and Gaelic Words in Shakspeare and his Contemporaries.

ALE DRAPER.

"A humorous term," says Nares, "for the keeper of an ale-house."

I came up to London, to be some tapster, hostler, or chamberlaine in an inn. Well, I get me a wife, with her a little money; when we are married, seek a house we must : no occupation have I, but to be an *ale draper*.

—CHETTLE, *Kind Hart's Dream* (1592).

Because 'thou hast not so much charity in thee as to go to the *ale* with a Christian :—Wilt thou go?

—*Two Gentlemen of Verona*, Act II. Sc. 5.

The word *Ale* is peculiar to the English language—and has long been erroneously supposed to have originated in the Saxon *aelan*, to kindle, to inflame, because of the intoxicating qualities of the liquor so called. But ale has not this quality in excess of other liquors, and in its origin simply meant *drink*, from the Keltic *ol*, drink or to drink; and *ol*, *olardh*, the act of drinking; *olar*, drunken, addicted to drink; and *olarachd*, habitual drunkenness. *Draper*, as used in the passage in *Kind Hart's Dream*, is the Keltic *druapair*, one who pours out or retails liquor in small quan-titles, also a tippler, whence *Ale Draper*, would signify one who sold drink by retail, whether it were wine, beer, ale, or spirits.

Nares, ignorant of the derivation, cites "*Ale*, the name of a rural festival," and adds, " where, of *course*, much *ale* was consumed."

There were bride *ales*, church *ales*, clerk *ales*, give *ales*, lamb *ales*, leet *ales*, Midsummer *ales*, scot *ales*, Whitsun *ales*, and several more.

—BRANDE's *Popular Antiquities.*

As will have been seen, the word *Ale* is used in *The Two Gentlemen of Verona* for "Ale-house." Bearing in mind the real etymology of *Ale*, it does not follow that in the church *ales*, bride *ales*, and others cited by Brande, that much or any *ale* was consumed, but only that some kind of drink was provided for the guests.

ARM-GAUNT.

This word is employed by Alexas when announcing to Cleopatra the approaching arrival of Antony :—

> He nodded
> And soberly did mount an *arm-gaunt* steed
> Who neighed so high, that what I would have spoke
> Was beastly dumb'd by him.
>
> —*Antony and Cleopatra,* Act I. Sc. 5.

When Antony mounted the "*arm-gaunt* steed," it neighed so loud in the pride of bearing such a noble burden that Alexas would not have heard his own voice if he had attempted to speak. The word has not been traced to any author but Shakspeare, and is usually considered a misprint. Hanmer suggested *arm-girt ;* Mason, *termagant ;* Boaden, *arrogant.* Nares asserts that " some will have it to mean *lean shoulder ;* some *lean* with poverty ; others *slender as one's arm ;* while

Warburton suggests, *worn by military service*. But these conjectures are all wide of the mark, for the idea of the poet was evidently to describe a gallant cavalier mounting a noble steed in triumph, and not bestriding a miserable hack ; and, as Nares adds, the explanations "are inconsistent with the speech which he made to display the gallantry of a lover to his mistress."

Boaden's conjecture of *arrogant*, would meet the sense, if the word as it stands is a misprint. But if it be printed as Shakspeare must be supposed to have written it, there is a Keltic etymology which would explain its meaning in *arm*, armour, and *gauntc*, bare or scanty ; so that *Arm-gaunt* would signify a horse without all or any of its martial trappings, on whose bare back Antony mounted in the pride of his strength and manhood, to present himself before the lady of his heart—exercising the completest mastery over his war-horse to gain favour in her eyes for his daring.

BILBOES.

Bilbo, a name for a sword supposed to have been manufactured at Bilboa in Spain, and to have derived its name from that city. The plural, *Bilbocs*, appears to have been the original designation of the implement, whatever it may have been, and to have been corrupted into *Bilbo*, when the first meaning had become obscure, in order to mark a distinction between the singular and the plural. The word has another and different signification in the shape of *Bilbo*, a place of confinement for cattle, to prevent them from straying. *Bilbo*, as a sword, or warlike weapon, has become wholly obsolete, but " in the *bilbocs*" is still a recognized phrase for imprisonment or captivity ; the words, though identical in sound, are not from the same source.

Shakspeare uses the word in both senses. In the *Merry Wives of Windsor*, Act. III. Sc. 5, Falstaff, who narrates his misadventure in the buckbasket, compares himself to a "good *bed*", in the circumference of a peck, hilt to point," that is, like a sword in its sheath. In *Hamlet*, Act V. Sc. 2, Hamlet says to Horatio :—

> Me thought I lay
> Worse than the mutineers in the *bilboes*.

Bilbo, in the sense of a sword or rapier ; has been too easily accepted by etymologists as taking its name from Bilboa. The first syllable, spelled usually *bill*, gives its name to many sharp instruments, among others to a kind of axe, halbert, or pike formerly carried by the English infantry, and afterwards by watchmen.

> Lo ! with a band of bowmen and of pikes,
> Brown *bills* and targeteers four hundred strong,
> I come.
>
> —*Edward II.* (Old Play).

A *bill* is also a kind of crooked hatchet, used by gardeners ; a hand-*bill*, a *bill*-hook, and a hedging-*bill* are similar instruments. A sword and a battle-axe were both called *bills*, so that the word may be considered a generic name for a sharp-cutting implement, whether employed for warlike or peaceful purposes. It is derived from the Keltic *buail*, to strike, to smite, to thrust, to stab. The second syllable, *bo*, abbreviated from *bos*, is from *bos*, the hand ; whence *Bilbo* a rapier, or small sword to be carried in the hand. It has been considered by Shak-spearean commentators, that the *Bilboes* (supposed to come from *Bilboa)* were famous for their fine tempered blades. In a note on the passage when Pistol in the first act of the *Merry Wives of Windsor* called Slender "a latten *bilbo*," Mr. Staunton explains that *latten* was a mixed metal akin to brass, and that the phrase means a sword wanting both edge and temper." As it is extremely unlikely that a sword blade was ever made of brass, it is most probable that *latten* was a misprint for *lathen*, or of *lathe*, referring to such a mock sword as that wielded by the harlequin of a pantomime.

Bilboes, as used by Hamlet, in the sense of an instrument or place of punishment, is a word of totally different origin. It is still in use among sailors, as in the lines of Charles Dibdin :—

> When in the *Bilboes* I was penn'd
> For serving of a worthless friend,
> And every creature from me ran,
> No ship performing quarantine
> Was ever so deserted seen ;
> None hailed me, woman, child, or man.

Mr. Halliwell says, " the *Bilboes* were a kind of stocks used at sea for the punishment of offenders " ; adding that " a wooden piece of machinery for confining the heads of sheep or cattle was formerly so called."

Here, again, the Keltic language supplies the etymology in *buaile*, a fold, a pen, a stall ; and *bo*, a cow ; whence *buaile bo*, or *Bilbo*, a cow-stall. The same language has *buaile-cach*, a stable or stall for horses.

B R A B E.

In *Cymbeline*, Act III. Sc. 3, Belarius, contrasting the meanness and the slavery of courts with the freedom and enjoyment of the country, says :—

> Oh ! this life
> Is nobler than attending for a *check*,
> Richer than doing nothing for a *babe*,
> Prouder then rustling in unpaid-for silk.

Johnson suggested that in this puzzling passage *babe* should be *brabe*, and Mr. Collier's annotator, *bab*. Hanmer reads it *bribe*, and Warburton *bauble*, which in old spelling was *Scene* Mr. G. Chalmers proposed *baubee*, the northern term for a half penny, and, according to Nares, spoke very contemptuously of the commentators for not adopting *it*. Mr. Staunton said that of all these emendations, the original *cue* being of course wrong, he preferred Hanmer's *bribe*, "though he had very little confidence even in that."

Johnson suggested the right word, though he either did not know or omitted to state its meaning. It does not occur in his own, or in any previous or subsequent Dictionary, not even in Halliwell's " Archaic," or Wright's " Provincial Glossary." *Brabe* is unquestionably the Keltic and Gaelic *breab*, a kick, a scornful repulse, a spurning; *breabirth*, kicking, from *breabach*, to kick; *brebadair*, a kicker. That this is the true meaning is evident from the context. It exactly fits the sense of the passage, "attending for a *check*," or a rebuff for doing nothing, only to receive a *kick*, or a repulse for attendance on the great. In what manner Johnson chanced upon the right word, does not appear.

CALEN O CUSTURE ME.

In *Henry V.*, Act IV. Sc. 4, Pistol, who has taken a prisoner from the French, exclaims to him "Yield, cur!" The prisoner, deprecating his wrath, says, in French, " I think you are a gentleman of good quality"; to which Pistol replies, "Quality, cality, construe me, Art *thou* a gentleman?" In the first Folio the words appeared as *Calmie custure me*, which were afterwards reprinted as *Call me, custure me*. This apparent jargon strongly puzzled all the commentators until Malone pointed out that he had met with an old Irish song (Gaelic) of which the burden and chorus was *Calen o custure me*. This was a clue to the enigma. Boswell afterwards found the tune in Playford's Collection, under the title of *Calino*, which has been reprinted by Mr. Chappell in his *Popular Music of the Olden Time;* and at greater length, including the words, by Mr. Samuel Lover, in the *Lyrics of Ireland* (1858). The full chorus is: "Callino, Callino, castore me. Eva ee, Eva ee, loo! loo! loo!" Boswell stated, on the authority of an Irish schoolmaster in London, that *Callino castore me*, signified in Gaelic, "Little girl of my heart, for ever and ever." This, however, is not the exact meaning. The words are a corrupt, but more or less phonetic, rendering of the Keltic *Caileno* (Irish-Gaelic, *Cailin*), a little girl; *ogh*, young (whence *callin o*), and *a stor mi*, my treasure; or, "little young girl, my treasure." A song, with a similar burden, is still known in the Highlands of Scotland, and has lately been republished in Sinclair's *Oranaiche*, or Book of Songs. The chorus ends: *Chailin og nach stiur thu mi*, which may possibly be the original; and would serve to prove that it was a boat-song, or *ramh-rann (refrain)*, from the words, *Stiur thu mi*, or, "Little young girl, steer me!" The words: "Eva ee, eva ee, loo! loo! loo!" as quoted by Mr. Lover, and not preserved in Shakspeare, are a corruption of *Aibhe i luaidh*, "Hail to her! the beloved one!"

The play of *Henry V.* was first performed in 1600, the year after the expedition of the Earl of Essex to Ireland, as appears from the evidence of the chorus to the fifth act :—

> Were now the general of our famous Empress
> (As in good time he may) from Ireland coming,
> Bringing rebellion broached on his sword,
> How many would the peaceful city quit
> To welcome him !

After their service in Ireland the disbanded soldiers of the army of Essex, who had caught the air and the words of the chorus from the Irish, brought the song into vogue among the populace of London, with whom Essex was as much a favourite as he was with the Queen (or Empress, as Shakspeare, as well as Spenser, called her). A further

proof that Keltic, or Gaelic, songs, or snatches of their
choruses, were sung in the streets of London in the later
years of the reign of Elizabeth, is afforded by Boswell, who
records a conversation with Dr. Johnson and Mr. Macqueen
on the subject, when in the Hebrides. The passage is
extracted from the Appendix to the *Gaelic Etymology of
the Languages of Western Europe, and more especially of the
English and Lowland Scotch* (London, 1877). "He (Johnson) said to Mr. Macqueen that he never could get the
meaning of an Erse Gaelic) song explained to him. They
told him the chorus was generally unmeaning. I take it,"
he added, "that Erse songs are generally like a song which
I remember. It was composed in Queen Elizabeth's time,
on the Earl of Essex, and the burthen was *Radarato,
Kadaratee, radara, tadara, tandoree*."—"But, surely," said
Mr. Macqueen, "there were words to it which had a
meaning?"—Johnson: "Why, yes, sir, I recollect a stanza,
and you shall have it":—

> Out then bespoke the 'prentices all
> Living in London, both proper and tall,
> For Essex's sake they would fight all
> *Radaratoo, radaratee, radara, tadara, tandoree.*

In this chorus the initial letter, G, has been dropped, and
the words ought to read :—

> Grad orra an diugh,
> Grad orra an de,
> Grad orra, teth orra,
> Tean do righe !

meaning :—

> Quick on them to-day !
> Quick on them as yesterday !
> Quick on them ! hot on them !
> Stretch forth thine arm !

This rendering has been adopted by Gaelic scholars ; and
the circumstance that such a ballad was sung in London

streets in the time of Elizabeth, throws light on the real
origin of Pistol's fag-end of a chorus, as quoted by Shakspeare. Mr. Staunton says that the Gaelic solution of the
difficulty is curious and captivating; but that to him the
idea of Pistol taking a Frenchman by the throat, and
quoting the fag-end of a ballad at the same moment, is too
preposterous. He, therefore, rejected the Gaelic interpretation, and adopted the reading of Warburton : "Quality,
cality, construe me, Art thou a gentleman ? " Mr. Staunton
was a judicious Editor, but he was wholly ignorant of the
Keltic sources of the English language.

CALF.

When the jealous Leontes in *A Winter's Tale* addresses
his little child Mamillius as a *calf*, it is not in derision, or
in depreciation either of himself or of the innocent boy of
whose paternity he is doubtful. "Art thou my *calf?*" he
asks, and Mamillius answers, "Yes, if you will, my Lord."
It is, perhaps, useless to enquire, after the lapse of three
centuries, whether *Calf* was a term of endearment to a child
among the English people ; but it is worthy of remark that
to the present day among the Keltic people of the Highlands of Scotland, and of the Gaelic-speaking population of
Ireland, *laogh*, which means a *calf*, or a fawn, is the very
fondest epithet that a mother can apply to her boy baby.
Mo laogh geal ('My white *calf*) is synonymous with My white,
my darling boy ; *Laogh mo cridhe, Calf* of my heart, is the
same as Darling of my heart. " Moon -*calf*," in old English,
was a phrase applied to a stupid child, and is used by Shakspeare in the *Tempest* in reference to " Caliban." "Moon " is
derived from *meunan*, to gape, to yawn in a stupid manner ;
whence " moon-*calf*" came to signify a stupid or silly child.
" Moon-raker," a word in the Slang Dictionaries, is from the
same root, with a derivation of " raker," from the Keltic

ig, obstinate: *i.e.*, an obstinate fool, a yawning, uncon-
vincible fool. The vulgar slang *kid*, a child, still in use,
is probably a remnant of the old vernacular which Shakspeare puts into the mouth of Leontes.—"Art thou my
only?" or "Art thou my *kid*?" from the Kymric. *Gid* and
goat are synonymous expressions.

CARRY COALS.

This phrase according to Nares signifies " to put up with
insults, to submit to any degradation." He asserts that
" the original meaning is, that in every family the scullions,
the turnspits, the carriers of wood and coals, were esteemed
the very lowest of menials. The latter in particular were
the *servi servorum*, the drudges of all the rest."

> Gregory ! o' my word we'll not *carry coals*.
>
> —*Romeo and Juliet*, Act I. Sc. 1.

> See, here comes one that will *carry coals;* ergo, will hold my dog.
>
> —BEN JONSON, *Every Man Out of Humour.*

Saxon philologists make a mistake in the meaning of
the word *Coals.* The common fuel for household use in
the days of Shakspeare and Ben Jonson was wood; and
though coal was partially known in England in the days of
James I., it was by no means in common use. Stowe the
annalist, writing in 1605, notices a peculiarity of the Scotch,
" that wood being scant and geason (scarce), they dug a
black stone out of the earth, which they burnt as fuel." If
Stowe had been familiar with the use of coal, and it had
been commonly known in England, he would not have
made such a remark as this in an historical work, that
treated of the manners and customs of his own time as well
as of previous ages. The word which in Shakspeare was
printed *Coal,* was probably the Keltic *cual,* from *cul,* the

back ; and *cual,* a heavy load of any material borne upon
the back ; whence *cualach,* heavy laden, and *cualag,* a small
load or burthen. The French have preserved the Keltic
word in *colis,* a portmanteau or travelling trunk, and *col-
porteur,* a pedlar carrying his goods upon his back.

In *Arden of Feversham,* sometimes, and perhaps correctly,
attributed to Shakspeare, appears the word *colestaff,* or
coltstaff, which Nares says " is a strong pole or staff on
which men carried a *burden* between them ; " adding, with
the idea of *coals* still running in his mind, " that the burden
was perhaps of that commodity." Burton, in his *Anatomie
of Melancholy,* speaks of witches who " ride in the ayre
upon a *coulstaffe.*"

CATAIAN.

This word, which Shakspeare uses twice, is, according to
Mr. Staunton, one of reproach, of which the precise mean-
ning is unknown. Mr. Halliwell and Mr. Wright say it
signifies a sharper. Nares defines it : " A Chinese, *Cathaia*
or *Cathay* being the name given to China by old travellers.
It was used for a sharper, from the desperate thieving of
those people, the Chinese."

I will not believe such a *Cataian,* though the priest of the town commended him for a true man.

— *Merry Wives of Windsor.*

" The opposition, in this passage," says Nares, " between
Cataian and *true,* or honest man, is a proof that it means
thief, or sharper, and Pistol is the person deservedly so
called."

It is possible, however, that all the commentators who
have tried to explain the mysterious word have been in error
in considering it to be a term of opprobrium or reproach ;
and that *Cataian* is no other than the old Keltic *cadain,* a
true friend from (*cad* a friend, and *ain,* honourable, just, true)

—a Warwickshire word, known to Shakspeare, though it appears to have been unknown to the literary and courtly circles of London. This sense of the word suits the intention of the speakers who use it. In the *Merry Wives of Windsor*, Pistol, Act II. Sc. 1, gives friendly information to Ford that Falstaff is in love with his wife; and Nym gives similar information to Page. Hence ensues the colloquy:—

Page. Here's a fellow (Nym) frights humour out of his wits.
Ford. I will seek out Falstaff.
Page. I never heard such a drawling, affecting rogue.
Ford. If I do find it, well.
Page. I do not believe such a *Cataian*, though the priest of the town commended him for a true man.

In this scene Ford inclines to believe that there may be truth in the friendly information given by Pistol, and afterwards by Nym, but Page is incredulous, and will not believe in the truth of such a friend, even though the priest of the town should vouch for and commend him. In like manner in *Twelfth Night*, Act II. Sc. 3, when Sir Toby Belch, Sir Andrew Ague-Cheek, and the Clown, are indulging in riotous merriment, and singing snatches of old songs and choruses in the Lady Olivia's house, the pert serving-maid Maria suddenly enters the room, exclaiming:—

What a caterwauling do you keep here! If my lady have not called up her steward, Malvolio, and bid him turn you out of doors, never trust me.

Sir Toby replies:—

My lady's a *Cataian*. Am I not consanguineous? am I not of her blood? that is to say, my lady will not do so. She is a good friend, and will not so behave to a blood relation.

Sir Toby Belch would not have used the word *Cataian* in reference to a lady of the high rank and importance of Olivia, if it really meant a thief or sharper. Possibly it was the application of the epithet to such a notoriously bad character as Pistol that led the commentators and etymologists astray as to the real meaning and origin of the word.

COLLOP.

Usually interpreted as a lump of flesh for cooking: a steak, a rasher of bacon, and sometimes minced meat, as in the dish called Scotch *Collops*. The word is derived by many philologists from the calf of the leg, as if a *Collop* were a piece of flesh taken from that part of the animal frame. Dr. Johnson adopts the derivation of Minshew from *coal*, and *up* or *upon*, i.e., flesh cooked upon the coal. Richardson traces it to *collow*, the smut of coal—on the principle apparently of *lucus a non lucendo*,—on the supposition that a lump of flesh cooked over the fire is sometimes blackened by the soot. Nares is somewhat scandalized at its use by the jealous Leontes, when he dubiously addresses his little child Mamillius in the *Winter's Tale* :—

> Come, Sir page !
> Look on me with thy welkin eye, sweet villain !
> Most dearest, my *collop !*

He remarks on this passage that " the metaphorical use of *Collop* by a father to his child as being part of his flesh, seems rather harsh and coarse." Shakspeare uses the word in the same sense in *Henry VIth* :—

> God knows thou art a *collop* of my flesh.

Nares, as if he doubted his previous interpretation, and would almost justify Shakspeare for his use of the word, remarks that Lyly certainly intended to be pathetic in the following passage :—

> The *collops* of thine own bowels to be the tortures of thine own soul.
> —*Mother Bombie*, Act I., Sc. 1.

The purely Keltic derivation of the word from *Colbh*, (pronounce Co'-*op* or co'-*op*), removes it from the vulgar interpretation of Nares and others, and places it in the poetic region to which it rightly belongs. *Colbh* signifies an offshoot, a sprout, a branch, a twig, a scion. The epithet was truly tender and pathetic in the mouth of Leontes, and not coarse, as Nares supposes. Its application to cookery, as in the phrase "a dish of *collops*," arose from a Saxon misapprehension of its meaning. A dish of *sprouts* or young sprouts of cabbage was afterwards applied to the more substantial fare of the flesh-eating Saxons, when butcher's-meat was mingled with the vegetables.

COSIER.

Malvolio says in *Twelfth Night*, "Do you make an ale-house out of my lady's house, that ye squeak out your *cosiers'* catches without any mitigation or remorse of voice?" What is a *Cozier*, or *Cosier*, as it is sometimes written? Dr. Johnson thought it meant a *tailor*, from *coudre* to sew. Nares and Halliwell considered it to mean a *cobbler;* while Harsnet, afterwards Archbishop of York, alludes to the catches or rounds sung by working people in ale-houses, and songs "sung by *tinkers* as they sit by the fire with a pot of good ale between their legs." The Keltic etymology of the word refers it neither to tinker, tailor, nor cobbler; but to *cos*, a foot, and *cosaire*, a traveller on foot, a walker, a pedestrian, a tramp; *cosan*, a footpath. It would thus appear that in Shakspeare's time, the working men of England, when on the tramp, or travelling from place to place in search of employment, were in the habit of assembling in the evening at the wayside public-houses, and to sing "rounds and catches" together. On this subject see Mr. Chappell's *Popular Music of the Olden Time*, Vol. I., pages 109, 110. The musical taste of the people was not confined to tailors, cobblers, or tinkers, as might be supposed by those who narrow the meaning of *Cosier*, to anyone handicraft, but prevailed generally among the working classes.

In the introduction to Boswell's *Journal of a Tour to the Hebrides* with Dr. Johnson, the editor (the late Dr. Carruthers of Inverness) says that at that time the last gleams of romance in Highland life had been extinguished, and that the chiefs no longer boasted of their *coshir*, or retinue, *i.e.*, their footmen, or men on foot, who followed them on grand occasions.

CRACK.

A small boy, a lively boy, a term of fondness.

Volumnia. One of his father's moods.
Valeria. Indeed! la' 'tis a noble child.
Virgilia. A *crack*, Madam.
　　　　　　　　　　　　　　　—Coriolanus, Act I. Sc. 4.

I saw him *crack* Skogan's head (talk ungrammatically) at the court-gate when he was a *crack*, not thus high.

　　　　　　　　　　—2nd Part of Henry IV., Act III. Sc. 2.

Since we are turned *cracks*, let us study to be like *cracks* : practise their language and behaviour ; act freely, carelessly, aud capriciously, as if one's veins ran quicksilver.

　　　　　　　—Ben Jonson, Cynthia's Revels, Act III. Sc. 1.

Mr. Staunton glosses *Crack* as a mannikin.

Nares is of opinion that the word signifies "one who *cracks* or boasts, a pert boy." Wright's "Dictionary of Obsolete and Provincial English" contains fifteen different meanings of *Crack*, of which the definition by Nares is one. It has, however, no relation to any one of the other fourteen, and is probably, as a term of endearment, a corruption of the Keltic *gradhach* (pronounced *crac* or *grac*), a beloved object, a little darling, a fondling boy. When used of a girl, the word is spelled *gradhag*, of almost identical sound.

CUTTLE.

In the second part of *Henry IV.*, Doll Tear-sheet threatens Pistol, on his assuming airs of undue familiarity with her :—

I'll thrust my knife into your mouldy chaps, if you play the saucy *cuttle* with me.

Nares is of opinion that *Cuttle* is a corrupted form of cutter, a bully, a swaggerer, a sharper. Mr. Halliwell seems to think that *Cuttle* is derived from the *cuttle*-fish, because in the same scene Doll Tear-sheet says : " Hang yourself, you mouldy *conger* (eel), hang yourself !" Nares rejects this derivation as too " refined " for Doll Tear-sheet. *Cuttle*, according to the " Archaic Dictionary " of Mr. T. Wright, was the knife used by thieves for cutting purses. But this explanation scarcely meets the sense of Doll's objurgation : " I'll thrust my knife into your chaps, if you play the saucy *knife* (*cuttle*) with me." The true derivation seems to be a corruption of the Keltic *cutalaiche*, a comrade, a bedfellow. This is a relationship to Pistol of which Doll Tear-sheet expresses her loathing and detestation, and is evidently the meaning if read by the light of her previous denunciation of his impudence in offering to *charge* or pay her for her favours. " Charge me ! I scorn you, scurvy companion, you poor, base, rascally, cheating, lack-linen mate ! Away, you mouldy rogue ! I am meat for your master." This at once explains Doll Tear-sheet's meaning and repugnance.

DISCANDY.

In *Antony and Cleopatra* (Act IV. Sc. 10), Antony, suspecting that Cleopatra has betrayed his fleet to Cæsar, and finding that his former friends and adherents are all abandoning him in his reverse of fortune, exclaims :—

> The hearts
> That *spaniel'd* me at heels, to whom I gave
> Their wishes, do *discandy*, melt their sweets
> On blossoming Cæsar.

On this extremely obscure and evidently corrupt passage, Nares remarks that "'hearts that *spaniel'd* Antony at heels, melting their sweets upon Cæsar,' is a masterpiece of incongruity." And such it undoubtedly is; but it would have been less obscure had not Hanmer first, and other commentators afterwards,—not understanding the words "*pannel'd* me at heels," as the phrase originally stood— altered *pannel'd* to *spaniel'd*. The Keltic word *pannel* or *bannal*, means a band, a troop, a company, an assemblage of men ; whence the modern English to *empanel* (or collect) a jury. The obvious meaning is "The hearts (men) that followed in troops, or crowds, at my heels have forsaken me to bestow their attentions upon Cæsar."

Cleopatra herself uses the word *Discandy* in the passionate imprecation to Heaven to turn her heart's blood to hail, if she have been cold-hearted to Antony, and let the first hail-storm fall upon her neck and kill her :—

> *Ant.* Cold-hearted towards me ?
> *Cleo.* Ah, dear, if I be so,
> From my cold heart let heaven engender hail,
> And poison it in the source ; and the first stone
> Drop in my neck : as it determines, so
> Dissolve my life ! The next Cæsarion smite !
> Till, by degrees, the memory of my womb,
> Together with my brave Egyptians all,
> By the *discandying* of this pelleted storm,
> Lie graveless,—till the flies and gnats of Nile
> Have buried them for prey !

The old copies read *discandering*, "from which corruption," Theobald says, he reformed the text to *discandy*. The final syllables, *candy*—signifying crystallized sugar, as in the modern sugar-candy, which could not possibly apply to the "hearts that *pannel'd* him"—led the commentators to imagine that *discandy* meant to un*candy*, to liquefy, to melt away or cause to melt away, like sugar-candy. "The idea," says Nares, ' is that as the stones of the hail melted, or *discandied*, a person should die for each." What seems to have strengthened this conjecture, are the words used by Antony after complaining that the "hearts" *melted their sweets* on blossoming Cæsar.

It would seem, however, on critical examination of these very obscure and confused passages, that neither *spaniel'd* nor *discandy* was used by Shakspeare, and that he meant and wrote *pannelled* and *discander*, as the words stood in the earliest editions.

Pannel'd has been already explained. *Discander* seems to have been a popular expression in Shakspeare's time, like *skedaddle* in ours, formed from the Keltic *dith* (*di*), to crowd or press together, and *sgannradh*, dispersion, a panic flight, a rout ; corrupted by the London compositors into *discander*, and allowed to pass unquestioned by the correctors of the press, and this gloss suits the exact sense of Antony's complaint of his followers ; and also of Cleopatra's allusion to the dispersing or passing away of the hail-storm ; the hardness, not the liquefaction of whose drops was to do the mischief. Perhaps in Antony's speech, "melt their *sweets*" should be read "melt their *suits*," *i.e.*, pour out their supplications, suits, and pleas for favour and advancement on the new potentate coming into power— the blossoming Cæsar ; *i.e.*, "the crowds that followed at my heels disperse in order to carry their suits to Cæsar the new dispenser of favour."

DUC DA ME.

This word, or phrase, occurs as a line in a stanza added by Jacques to a song sung by Amiens in *As You Like It:*—

> If it do come to pass
> That any man turn ass,
> Leaving his wealth and ease
> A stubborn will to please,
> *Duc da me, Duc da me,*
> Here shall he see
> Gross fools as he.

Amiens, puzzled by the phrase *Duc da me,* asks Jacques what it means. Jacques replies, "'Tis a Greek invocation, to call fools into a circle." By "Greek" he appears to have meant "*Pedlar's Greek*"—the popular name for slang or for the cant language of the beggars and gipsies of his day, which is not wholly disused in our own. In a note on this passage, Mr. Staunton says, "After all that has been written in elucidation of the word, we are disposed to believe that it is mere unmeaning babble coined for the occasion." Sir Thomas Hanmer and others thought it was once a call of farm-wives and farm servants when summoning the ducks to be fed !

No one has discovered, or even hinted at, the "circle" to which Jacques alludes. Perhaps the old game of Tom Tidler's Ground may throw some light on the matter. One of the most ancient of the rhymes still sung by British children is—

> Here I am on Tom Tidler's ground,
> Picking up gold and silver.

The origin and meaning of the name *Tom Tidler* have given rise to much controversy. The Rev. E. Cobham Brewer, in his "Dictionary of Phrase and Fable," maintains it to be a corruption of "Tom th' Idler." "Tom," he says,

" in the game stands on a heap or mound of stones, gravel,
&c." Other boys rush on the heap, crying, " Here I am on
T m Tidler's Ground," &c. " *Tom* bestirs himself to keep
the invaders off." This has hitherto passed muster, but the
true derivation is from the Keltic, or Gaelic, proving the
game to have been known to British children before the
Saxon and Danish irruption and conquest. *Tom* signifies
" hill " or mound, a word that enters into the composition
of the names of many places in the British Isles ; and *tiod-
lach*, gift, offering, treasure : so that *Tom-tiodlach*—corrupted
by the Danes and Saxons into *Tom-tiddler*—signifies " the
hill of gifts or treasure," of which the players seek to hold
or to regain possession. It was the custom for the boy who
temporarily held the hill or *tom* to assert that the ground
or circle belonged to him of right, and dare the invaders
to dispossess him, by the exclamation of *Duc da mé.* This
phrase has puzzled commentators quite as much as the
name of *Tom Tidler* has done. The word, however, resolves
itself into the Keltic, or Gaelic, *Duthaich*, the *t* silent before
the aspirate (pronounced *du-haic*), and signifying a country,
an estate, a territory, a piece of land ; *do* signifying to, and
mi me—*i.e.*, this territory or ground is to me ; it is my land
or estate. This old British phrase continued to be used
by children and illiterate people long after the British
language had given way to the Saxon English, and was
repeated by boys and girls in the game now called *Tom
Tidler's* Ground so lately as forty years ago, when I heard
it used by children on the Links of Leith and the Inchs
of my native city of Perth.

Tom, in the Scottish Highlands and in the Irish Gaelic
still spoken in the West of Ireland, signifies either a hill or
a thicket ; and *tiodhlac* a gratuity, a largess, a boon ; and
du-aic land, possession, estate, country.

FINCH EGG.

The meaning of this epithet, applied by Thersites, the filthy railer, to Patroclus in *Troilus and Cressida*, is, as Nares remarks, "by no means clear, though evidently meant as a term of reproach."

> *Patroclus.* You indistinguishable cur !
> *Thersites.* Why art thou, then, exasperate, thou idle immaterial skein of sleyd silk, thou green sarsnet flap for a sore eye ! thou tassel of a prodigal's purse, thou ? Ah, how the poor world is pestered with such waterflies !
> *Patroclus.* Out ! gall !
> *Thersites.* Finch Egg.

Steevens says that "A *finch's egg* is remarkably gaudy, and that the word may thus be equivalent to a coxcomb." "But," remarks Nares, "the chaffinch, bulfinch, and goldfinch have all eggs of a bluish-white, with purplish spots or stripes." And he thence implies that these eggs are not gaudy, and that the simile is inappropriate. It may perhaps throw some light on the subject, if we consider that the Keltic *fincag* or *fionag* signifies a mite, an animalcule, a maggot, a contemptible insect, and that *Finch* is probably a corruption of that word. Thus, Thersites after having exhausted all the abusive epithets at his immediate command, wound up by calling Patroclus a maggot's egg, than which nothing could be smaller or more contemptible.

GONERIL, REGAN, AND CORDELIA.

The story of King Lear and his three daughters belongs to the Keltic period of British history or tradition. King *Leir*, as the name is written in the old chronicles, is supposed to have been the son of Bladud, and to have reigned over part of Britain in the middle of the ninth century before the Christian era. Shakspeare did not invent the legend on which he founded his matchless tragedy, nor the names of the three daughters of the unhappy king, all of which he found recorded in Geoffrey of Monmouth, and other ancient chroniclers. It has never before been pointed out that their purely Keltic names are descriptive of the characters assigned to each of the three sisters in the old legend. *Goneril* is derived from *gon*, a wound, and *gonach*, sharp, keen, cruel, wounding, stinging, and *riaghail*, to rule or govern: *Regan* from *righinn*, hard, stubborn, unyielding, unbending; and *Cordelia*, from *cord*, agreement, or to agree or *carr*, excellent, and *dileach*, loving, affectionate. No reader of Shakspeare can fail to recognise the singular accuracy of the epithets as applied to the three women, or by what easy transitions of pronunciation from the Keltic to the Saxon the words acquired the form which they now bear. *Leir* or *Leire* signifies in Keltic, austere and pious; and it is possible that the ancient king, if he ever existed, was so named by his contemporaries, in designation of his character.

GONGARIAN.

In the scene in the first act of the *Merry Wives of Windsor*, when Bardolph is recommended to accept service as tapster to "mine host of the Garter," Falstaff says :—

Bardolph, Follow him : a tapster is a good trade. An old cloak makes a new jerkin, a withered serving-man a fresh tapster ! Go ! adieu !

and Pistol in disgust at Bardolph's acquiescence in the arrangement exclaims—

O base *Gongarian* wight ! wilt thou the spigot wield !

Nares supposes that *Gongarian* is a corruption of *Hungarian*—"perhaps to make a more tremendous sound"; but why *Hungarian*, he does not explain. It is clearly *Gonga-rian* in the first Quarto. If the word be derived, as is probable, from the Keltic *gon*, to cut, to slash, to carve ; and *gaorran*, a glutton, the phrase would mean that Bardolph was about to add to the gluttony of a greedy wielder of the carving-knife the drunkenness of a wielder of the spigot. *Hungarian*, according to Mr. Halliwell, is an old cant term, generally meaning an hungry person, but sometimes a thief or rascal of any kind. Of the two words, *Gongarian*, in the Keltic sense, is preferable in force of expression, the more especially as the correction, if it be a correction, into *Hungarian*, was not made by Shakspeare.

HACK.

In the *Merry Wives of Windsor*, Act II. Sc. 1, we find what Nares calls a "puzzling speech." Mrs. Ford says to Mrs. Page : "If I would but go to hell for an eternal moment, or so, I could be *knighted*." Mrs. Page replies : "What !—thou liest !—Sir Alice Ford ?—These knights will *hack ;* and so thou shouldst not alter the quality of thy gentility.

Nares is of opinion that *Hack* meant cut or chop, and that Shakspeare used it as an appropriate term for chopping off the spurs of a knight, when he was to be degraded. But if this were truly the etymology of the word, we might ask whether *Hack* was both an active and a passive verb, and whether *Hack* signified *to be hacked*. Nares adds, in explanation, "One lady (Mrs. Ford) had said she might be knighted, alluding to her offered connection with Falstaff. Mrs. Page, not yet knowing her meaning, says, in effect : 'What ! a female knight ! These knights will degrade such unqualified pretenders.'" This explanation is supported by the not very great authority of Dr. Johnson. As there is no known authority for the use of the word

Hi ' for the degradation of a knight, and as knights of
th calibre and quality of Sir John Falstaff could degrade
nobody but themselves, further search ought to be made for
its meaning, though Nares was decided that nothing else
could be made of it. Mr. Staunton is of opinion that no
satisfactory explanation of the word *Hack* has ever been
given. "It is generally understood," he adds, "to be an
allusion to the extravagant creation of knights by James I.,
in the early part of his reign—'These knights will *hack*,
or become *hacknied*.'" But as the *Merry Wives* was written
in the reign of Elizabeth, the allusion is an anachronism,
even if the etymology were otherwise well-founded. Mr.
Staunton is quite correct in his opinion "that there must
be a meaning in it more pertinent than this."

In the local dialects of England *hack*, or *hag*, has various
meanings besides that of cut or hew. In the glossary to
Tim Bobbin (Lancashire dialect), *hack* signifies to knock
together; and in Halliwell's "Archaic Dictionary," *hack* has
no less than twelve different meanings :—1. A pick-axe, a
hoe ; 2. a hatch or half door ; 3. to stammer or cough faintly ;
4. a place to dry newly made bricks ; 5. the entrails of
swine ; 6. a hard-working man ; 7. *hack* at, to irritate;
8. a place where a hawk's food was set for it ; 9. to hop on
one leg ; 10. to chatter with cold ; 11. a hedge ; 12. to win
anything ; and *hag* or *hack*, to dispute, whence *haggle* over
a bargain. Mr. Thomas Wright's " Provincial Dictionary "
also contains these words, but none of them seems to meet
the sense. A meaning can be found in the Keltic vernacular, in the use of which Shakspeare was a proficient ;
in which language *ac* or *acaidh* signifies to deny, to repudiate. So that what Mrs. Page probably meant, was:
" These knights [such as Falstaff] will deny that they have
made you 'Sir Alice' [or 'Lady' Alice], after they have
deceived you and made you alter the quality of your
gentility by having anything to do with them." All Keltic
words that begin with a vowel are aspirated—so that *ac*

becomes *hac*, the English *hack*. The Gaelic Dictionary published under the auspices of the Highland Society of Edinburgh defines *ac* or *ag* as denial, repudiation.

Under the word *Hackster* or *Haxter*, Nares, still misled by his previous idea of *hackney*, affirms that *hackster* means a hacknied person, and quotes :—

To bring an old *hackster* to the exercise of devotion is to bring an old bird to sing prick song in a cage.

—BRAITHWAITE'S *Whimsies.*

Here the sense would be correctly rendered by the Keltic *ac*, to deny, to repudiate. A *hackster* returning to his devotions, signifies one who has previously denied or repudiated his religion.

JAKES.

Jakes,—a water-closet—a place of convenience, formerly called in French a *commodité.*

Your lion that holds his poll-axe, sitting
On a close stool, will be given to *A-jax:*
He will be the ninth worthy.

—*Love's Labour Lost*, Act V. Sc. 2.

The name of the ancient hero *Ajax*, nearly the same in sound as the once common word a *jakes*, furnished, says Nares, many unsavoury puns to our ancestors. "The etymology," he adds, "is uncertain, unless we accept the very bad pun of Sir John Barrington (who wrote the *Metamorphosis of Ajax*) who derives it in jest from an old man, who, at such a place, cried out '*age aches.*'" This vulgar and ridiculous derivation has been hitherto sufficient for Saxon philologists, but the Keltic provides the true etymology in *deic* (pronounced *jake*) convenient, and *deicheas*, conveniency, or a place of conveniency. From *a jake*, in the singular, came the corruption *a jakes*, and the still more foolish corruption, *Ajax*.

LAMB.

This word occurs in the quarrel scene between Brutus and Cassius in the fine tragedy of *Julius Cæsar*. Cassius, stung by the reproaches of Brutus, bares his breast, and draws his dagger, inviting Brutus to take his heart, instead of gold, which he had denied him. Brutus replies :—

> Sheathe your *dagger*.
> Be angry when you will, it shall have scope !
>
> .   .   .   .
>
> O Cassius, you are yokèd with a *lamb*,
> That carries anger as the flint bears fire ;
> Which much enforcèd, shows a hasty spark,
> And straight is cold again.

Sufficient critical acumen has not been brought to bear upon the expression "*yoked* with a *lamb*." Yoked has been held to mean coupled ; and Brutus is supposed to assert that he himself is of a lamb-like nature ; and that his anger, provoked by Cassius, his yoke-fellow, is as transient as the spark of a flint. Mr. Staunton, who seems to acquiesce in the interpretation, objects nevertheless to the word *lamb*, which, he observes, " can scarcely have been Shakspeare's word. Pope, who saw its unfitness, printed *man* ('instead of *lamb*), but it requires a happier conjecture than this to justify an alteration of the text."

Man is certainly no better than *lamb* as a clue to Shakspeare's meaning, and a justification of his simile to the flint. It is probable, however, that in this, as in so many other instances, the clear meaning of Shakspeare has been darkened by his ignorant printers. Mr. Halliwell says, *Lamm*, is a plate or scale of metal, and that it is an armourer's term. Nares quotes from Sidney's *Arcadia* :— " He strake Phalantus just upon the gorget, so as he battered the *lamms* thereof," and derives the word, which he says means a plate, from the Latin, *lamina*.

The French *lame* signifies the blade of a sword, of a

dagger, of a knife, &c., and this apparently was the word, pronounced *lamm*, which Shakspeare employed, and which his printers corrupted into *lamb*. The root of the word is the Keltic *lann*, whence the French and English *lance*, a spear; but in Keltic signifying the same as the French *lame*, the sharp blade of an offensive or defensive weapon. Thus it was the *dagger*, or *lame* (blade), of Cassius, which he had just unsheathed that provoked the taunting remark of Brutus as to its harmlessness. The suggested emendation restores the true sense and poetry of the passage. The change of the Keltic terminal *n* into *m* in English, Lowland Scotch, and French, in words borrowed from the more ancient language, is common, as in the vulgar word *bum*, from *bun*, a fundament, or foundation; and *Dum*barton, from *Dun*barton. As regards *yoke* in this passage which Johnson cites as signifying coupled, as if Cassius and Brutus were coupled together, it means " burthened," and the true sense is :—" O Cassius you are burthened with a *lamm* (weapon, dagger, blade, etc.)," as in the Scriptural phrase, " My *yoke* is easy, and my burthen is light."

LAMB'S WOOL.

The name of a drink in the seventeenth century, described in Nares and in many old authors. This phrase is a striking exemplification of the fact that the Keltic words which remained in the vernacular long after their original meaning had been lost, were continually subjected to a Saxon pronunciation and interpretation which did not belong to them. This is more especially the case in the matter of drinks. Thus, *ol taom* (the drink to pour out) was metamorphosized into " Old Tom," still the favourite name for gin. *Deoch nos*, signifying the usual drink, became " dog's nose " ; *Deoch an dingh* (a drink to-day), became " Dog and Duck," still a familiar sign for public-houses; and *sean deoch* (*shan deoch*), the "old drink," was perverted into *shandy-gaff*, which word an egregious pundit of our time asserts to have been derived from one Goff, a blacksmith, to whom this liquor was as dear as his heart's blood; and that *shandy-gaff* was named in his honour "Sang de Goff"!

Lamb's Wool was a drink composed of ale and the pulp of apples, thoroughly mixed by continuous hand labour, until the beverage became of a perfectly smooth consistency. The liquor is mentioned by Peele, a contemporary of Shakspeare, and by Herrick, who lived a little later :—

> Lay a crab-apple in the fire, to roast for *lamb's wool.*
>
> *Old Wives' Tale*—PEELE.

> Now crown the bowl
> With gentle *lamb's wool,*
> Add sugar, and nutmeg, and ginger.
>
> —HERRICK.

The old Keltic name was *lamh's suil*, hand and eye, so named from the labour of the hand required to make the *purée* of apples smooth and without lumps in the liquor, and the eye to perceive and approve of the results. *Lamh* is the hand; *'s* is the contraction of *agus* (and); whence *lamh's suil*, perverted into the Saxon English *Lamb's Wool.*

LAND-DAMN.

This word, or combination of words, is used in the *Winter's Tale*. Its meaning has excited much controversy, without leading to any satisfactory explanation. Antigonus says to Leontes, who doubts the honour of his wife :—

> You are abused, and by some putter-on
> That will be *damned* for it! Would I knew the villain,
> I would *land-damn* him !

Here a pun is evidently intended—the villain shall not
only be *damned* but *land-damned.* Mr. Staunton says
that the passage "may almost with certainty be pronounced corrupt," and adds, "that the only tolerable
attempt to extract sense from it, is that of Rann, who
conjectured that it meant condemned to the punishment
of being built up in the earth, a torture mentioned in
Titus Andronicus,—" Set him breast deep in the earth,
and famish him."

"Dr. Johnson," says Nares, "interprets *Land-damn* as, 'I
will *damn* him, or condemn him, to quit the *land*.' Sir
Thomas Hanmer derives it from *lant*, urine; and explains
it, 'To stop his urine, which he might mean to do by total
mutilation'; and there is this to be said in favour of his
explanation, that it suits with the current and complexion
of the whole speech, which is gross with the violence of
passion, and contains indecent images of a similar kind."
He adds that Dr. Farmer's conjecture of "'laudanum him,'
in the sense of to poison him, has no probability to recom-
mend it."

Mr. Wedgwood, in *Notes and Queries*, states his opinion
that *Land-damn* ought to be read *landann;* adding, "It is
hardly doubtful that *landan*, like randan, or rantan, is a
mere representation of continued noise. The name of
landan was given, in the Midland Counties, to a *charivari*
of rough music, by which country people were accustomed,
as late as forty years ago, to express their indignation
against some social crime, such as slander or adultery.'
But this is scarcely satisfactory. Possibly in an earlier
time the popular indignation displayed itself in a more
vigorous manner than by rough music, and took the shape
of rough blows. *Land-damn* is not a corruption of *landan*,
but *landan* is a corruption of the older word, of which the
roots are the Gaelic *lann*, the penis or pizzle of an animal;
and *damh*, a bull, or stag; whence *lann-damh*, a bull's
pizzle, which, when dried, was converted into a scourge of

a formidable nature. Thus, " I will *damn* him, and *land-damn* him," signifies, with a grim pun in the phrase, " I will damn him, aye, and scourge him also with a bull's pizzle." The word *pizzle*, as a *scourge*, occurs in Bailey's Dictionary, 1731.

M A L T - H O R S E.

From the sense of the two passages in which this word is used by Shakspeare, it is evidently a term of reproach :—

> Mome ! *Malt-horse !* capon ! coxcomb ! idiot ! patch !
> —*Comedy of Errors*, Act III. Sc. 1.

> You peasant swain ! you whoresom *malt-horse !*
> —*Taming of the Shrew*, Act IV. Sc. 1.

Mr. Halliwell quotes the word *Malt-mare*, employed in a similar sense :—

> He would simper and snuffle as though he had gone a-wooing to a *malt-mare !'*
> —LILLY (1632).

The conjunction of the words *malt* and *horse* has suggested to some commentators that it means a brewer's horse. Nares says that " *malt* horses were probably strong *heavy* horses, like dray horses." Mr. Halliwell is of the same opinion, and says that " *malt*-horse, is a *slow, dull, heavy* horse, such as is used by brewers." It may be questioned, however, whether *malt*, in this phrase, means the malt from which brewers make beer, or that a brewer's horse, though strong, is necessarily dull or stupid because he is less agile than a race-horse. The obvious English word too easily satisfied the English etymologists. The Welsh, or Kymric, branch of the Keltic languages spoken in the British Isles, supplies *mallt*, which in all the Welsh dictionaries is explained as " devoid of energy, dull, spiritless, stupid." The

Gaelic branch has *mall*, slow; and *maol* or *maoladh*, dull, heavy, blunt, which supports Mr. Halliwell's derivation. Thus, *Malt-horse* as used by Shakspeare does not mean the horse that draws the malt for the brewer; but a dull, heavy, stupid horse—whether he belonged to a brewer, or to any other person.

MARR, OR MAR.

In Antony's spirit-stirring address to the citizens of Rome, over the dead body of Cæsar, he says, exhibiting the dagger stabs in his garment :—

> Kind souls, what, weep you when you but behold
> Our Cæsar's vesture wounded? Look you here,
> Here is himself, *marr'd*, as you see, with traitors.

The ordinary meaning of *Mar*, to spoil, to disfigure, does not meet the sense of the passage. If it were intended to convey that Cæsar was *marred*, or spoiled, it would be *by* and not *with* traitors. The author of a recent glossary of the archaic words of the county of Stafford, has a note on the passage, in which he states that *mar*, in Staffordshire, signifies spoilt, used of a child; which *Notes and Queries*, of September 18th, 1880, remarks is not a good illustration. It may be suggested that the Keltic word *mar*, which means, like, similar, the same, is, in all probability, the solution of the difficulty, as if Antony had said, " Here is Cæsar himself, and not merely his vesture, treated as if he were a traitor to the Commonwealth." This allegation it is the whole purpose of his eloquent speech to repudiate and deny. From this word comes the Lowland Scotch *marrow*, in the sense of a pair, as in the expression, " These gloves are no *marrows*," *i.e.*, they are not a pair—" His een are no *marrows*," *i.e.*, he squints, his two eyes are not alike. A Lowland Scotsman would make the

passage quite intelligiible if he read it, "Here is himself
marrow'd, or paired, as you see, with *traitors*." Ben Jonson
uses *marrow* in the sense of a companion, or mate.

MEAL-MOUTHED.

The modern *mealy-mouthed* was written and pronounced
meal-mouthed in the sixteenth and seventeenth centuries:—

> Who would imagine yonder sober man,
> The same devout, *meale-mouthed* precisian,
> That cries good brother, kind sister, and
> Is a vile politician?
>
> > MARSTON'S *Satires* (1598).

> Ye hypocrites,
> Ye *meale-mouthed* counterfeits.
>
> > HARMAN'S *Beza (quoted by Nares)*.

Nares says : " This word is applied to one whose words
are as fine and soft as *meal*, as Minshew well explains it."
Johnson, on the same track, says, " Imagined by Skinner to
be corrupted from *mild*-mouthed or *mellow*-mouthed ; but
perhaps from the *sore mouths of animals*, that when they
are unable to comminute their grain, must be fed with
meal." *Meal* is not always soft in the mouth, but sometimes gritty, and more or less rough. A much more
probable derivation is from the Keltic *milis*, soft, sweet ;
mil, honey. Shakspeare has *honey*-mouthed and *honey*-
tongued, as in :—

> A *honey* tongue—a heart of gall,
> Is Fancy's Spring, but Sorrow's Fall.

This derivation is so obvious that it seems strange that any
philologist should miss it, or prefer *meal*, ground grain, to
mil, honey, as the origin of the simile. But English philologists like to travel in the old ruts, and, knowing nothing
of Keltic, prefer Saxon resemblances to Keltic realities.

MEINY—MENIE.

A household, and the people composing it;—the French *menage.*

> A reeking post
> Delivered letters—(from Goneril)
> Which presently they read, and whose contents
> They summoned up their *meiny*, straight took horse,
> Commanded me to follow.
>
> —*King Lear.*

Mr. Staunton explains *Meiny* in this passage to mean a "retinue," in which sense it is used in Stowe's *Survey*, who says the guests "were set and served plentifully with venison and wine by Robin Hood and his *meynie*." It is a mistake to derive this word from the same source as *many*, the plural of *much*. In the "Dictionnaire de la Langue Romane, ou vieux langage Français" (Paris, 1768), *mesnie* or *mesnies*, is explained as signifying "habitations, fermes, bourgs, et villages." The word is used in the Scottish Lowland dialect as *mains*, a farm and collection of farm buildings. Halliwell's "Archaic Dictionary" (1848), states that "*meny*, a family," is a word still in use in the North of England. It is from the old Keltic *muinn* or *muinne*, the people comprising the household, the servants and retainers of a chief; whence *muinntir*, a large farm or establishment —and *muinntireach*, largely provided with servants, having a numerous household.

MEPHISTOPHELES.

This word, rendered more familiar to the last and present generations by the *Faust* of Goethe, was known in the Elizabethan era, and used by Shakspeare and Marlowe a century and a half before Goethe. In its present orthography, it has all the appearance of a Greek word; but the Greek knows it not. In the Shaksperean era it was written *Mephistophilis* and *Mephistophilus*—

> Come, *Mephistopholis*, let us dispute again,
> And argue of divine astrology !
>
> —MALONE.

Hath *Mephistopholis* no greater skill—
Who knows not the double motion of the planets ?

—*Ibid.*

Pistol, in *Merry Wives of Windsor*, Act I. Sc. 2, uses the word jocularly—

How now, *Mephistophilus ?*

Nares describes the word as a fanciful name of a supposed familiar spirit mentioned in the old legend of *Sir John Faustus*. It appears to have been compounded of two Keltic words—*mi-fios*, mis-knowledge or perversion of knowledge; and *diabhol (dia-vol)*, devil; whence *mi-fios-diathol*, the devil of perverted or misleading knowledge— an exact description of the cunning devil pourtrayed by Marlowe and Goethe.

MERRY ANDREW.

Merry Andrew is an old word of the Elizabethan era for a jester, or mountebank, not yet wholly obsolete. Johnson is the first English lexicographer who notices it, and translates it a Jack-pudding, a buffoon. He attempts no etymology. The Germans call a *Merry Andrew* a " Jack Sausage," or *Hans Würz*. The French call it *saltinbanque*, and *Jean Potage*. A writer in *Notes and Queries*, Feb. 7th, 1852, says : " Although Strutt in his *Sports and Pastimes* has several allusions to *Merry Andrews*, he does not attempt to explain the origin of the term. Hearn, in his *Benedictus Albus*, speaking of the well-known Andrew Borde, gives it as his opinion that this facetious physician gave rise to the name; 't was from the Doctor's method of using such speech at markets and fairs, that in after times those that imitated the like humorous, jocose language were styled *Merry Andrews*, a term much in use among our stages."

All the lexicographers who mention the word, which is one peculiar to the English language, are content to derive it from this Dr. Andrew Borde. The true root seems to be the Keltic *mear*, merry; *mir*, to sport; *mearaiche*, a clown, a buffoon; *mirean*, sportiveness; combined with *druidh* (pronounced *Droo-i*), a conjuror, a pretended magician. We have thus the common word *Merry Andrew*, without reference to the fabulous physician, whom lazy makers Dictionaries, each following in the track of his prede-cessors, are contented to accept. Thus we have *An druidh bord*, a jesting conjuror. *Bord*, in Keltic, signifies a jest, a witticism, a joke, as in the lines quoted by Nares :—

> Trust not their words
> Nor merry *bords*.
>
> —DRAYTON.

MERRY GREEK.

This phrase occurs twice in *Troilus and Cressida*, and is once the occasion of a pun by the fair and fickle Cressida [Act I. Sc. 2]. In reply to Pandarus, who thinks that Helen loves Troilus better than she does Paris, she replies jestingly, "Then she is a *merry Greek* indeed." Mr. Staunton remarks that "*Merry Greek* meant a wag or humourist, and is frequently to be met with in old books. Our oldest English comedy, *Ralph Roister Doister*, has a character who is the droll of the piece, called Ma the w *Merry-Greeke*." Mr. Staunton attempts no etymology, and gives no explanation why in England the Greeks, if the

would be derived from that nation, should be considered
merrier than other people, or than the inhabitants of
"Merry England," to whom the pleasant epithet was usually
applied. *Mir* in Keltic signifies sportive, joyful, wanton,
and from that language the English words merry and
merriment are derived. *Greek*, in this particular phrase,
derived from the Keltic *cridhe* (cree), the heart, and *crid-
leac* (pronounced *cree-ach*), hearty, pleasant; whence *Merry
Greek* corrupted from *meare-cridheach*, merry-hearted.

MODERN.

Shakspeare, in several instances, makes use of this word
in a sense which is not that of *modern*, as opposed to
antique; and which all the commentators agree in considering must mean, trivial, worthless, common. The most
noted example occurs in *As You Like It*, Act II. Sc..7, in
the line :—

> Full of wise saws, and *modern* instances ;

in which *modern*, as opposed to *antique*, is generally accepted as the true meaning : " Full of ancient sayings or
proverbs, and modern instances of their wisdom." In the
following instances, among many others that might be
cited, a similar interpretation cannot be held valid. When
Rosalind tells the melancholy Jacques that those who
indulge in extremity of either laughter or melancholy—

> Betray themselves to every *modern* censure,
> As worse than drunkards,

modern, as distinguished from *ancient*, is wholly inappli-
cable.

So in *Macbeth*, Act. IV. Sc. 3 :—

> Where sighs, and groans, and shrieks that rend the air,
> Are made, not mark'd ; where violent sorrow seems
> A *modern* ecstasy—

modern in the usual sense is clearly inadmissible. The same remark applies to the Queen's speech in *Antony and Cleopatra*, Act. V. Sc. 2 :—

> Say, good Cæsar,
> That I some lady trifles have reserved,
> Immoment toys, things of such dignity
> As we greet *modern* friends withal.

The Keltic *modhar* signifies gentle, mild, soft, in which sense in the passages above quoted *gentle* might be substituted for *modern*, with the greatest advantage to the meaning. The same interpretation would exactly suit the passage in Ben Jonson's *Poetaster* :—

> Alas ! that were no *modern* consequence
> To have cothermal briskness frightened hence.

NIGHTMARE.

In *King Lear*, Act. III. Sc. 4, Edgar quotes what is supposed to be a passage from an old song :—

> Saint Withold footed thrice the wold ;
> He met the *night-mare* and her nine-fold ;
> Bade her alight,
> And her troth plight,
> And aroint thee, witch, aroint thee !

This doggerel is evidently corrupt, and some annotators have endeavoured to make sense of the second line by reading " The *night-mare* and her nine *foals*." The emendation, however, only helps to make the confusion worse confounded ; although the nine " foals " of a mare, supposing the delirium of sleeplessness, or perturbed sleep in the night, to be rightly personified in the shape of a female horse, as the superstitious and vulgar notion is, are comprehensible enough. In French, the word which the English renders " mare " is *mar*, which does not signify a female horse.

The French call the Nightmare the "couche-mar," in which the final syllable would have to be *jument*, and not *mar*, if the received English etymology were correct, or the English interpretation prevailed in France. The word *Nightmare* in English results from a misunderstanding of the ancient Keltic *mear*, which signifies delirium: plural *mearan*; whence *Nichd mear*, corrupted into " Night-*mare*," the delirium of the night. Many philologists, aware of the absurdity of the derivation from the female horse supposed to sit on the bosoms of sleepless persons, have sought to trace the word from the Runic and Teutonic *mar* (or *mur*), a demon or incubus, which, according to Malone, had nine families. Not one of them, however, has discovered the simple and obvious Keltic etymology that makes an end of the *mare* and her "nine-*fold*" or *foals*, and brings down the superstitious fancy to the level of common-sense, and to a plain prose description neat enough to be accepted as scientific by any physician who understands the causes of the temporary malady.

PASH.

In *Winter's Tale*, Act I. Sc. 2, Leontes, suspicious of the fidelity of his wife, Hermione, addresses his little son, Mamillius, and asks :—

> Art thou *my* calf?
> *Mamillius.* Yes, if ye will, my lord.
> *Leontes.* Thou want'st a rough *pash* and the shoots that I have,
> To be full like me.

"Calf" in this passage was probably at one time in the English vernacular a term of peculiar endearment for a young child—as it remains to this day, among the Gaelic-speaking people of Scotland. A Highland mother has no more affectionate words for her baby boy than *Mo laoch* (my calf).

Nares thought that the word *Pash* meant something belonging to a calf or bull, and that it was probably a provincial word that had not been traced out, adding that Steevens pretended to derive it from *paz*, a kiss in Spanish, a derivation for which there was neither proof nor probability. Grose mentions " mad-*pash* " as meaning a madcap in Cheshire. Mr. T. Wright says that in the same county *Pash* means brains; and Mr. Staunton, who, though ignorant of the Keltic languages, came very near the mark in this instance, explained *Pash* as a tufted head or brow. The word in reality means the forehead, and is the English rendering of the Gaelic *bathais* (pronounced *bash* or *pash*, *b* and *p* being interchangeable in that language), signifying the brow or forehead. The word *abash*, in its sense of to browbeat or intimidate, is from the same root. Thus, in the speech of the forlorn Leontes to the innocent child, whom he suspects may not be his own, a " rough *pash* " means a brow furrowed with care, like his father's, and the " shoots " the emblematic horns which the jealous husband is afraid he wears.

If this had been known to the Rev. Alexander Dyce, one of the many ignorant and pretentious editors of Shakspeare, he would not have fallen into the ludicrous error common to him, to Malone and others, of supposing that Leontes compared himself to a bull, the sire of a calf. Malone, in attempting to explain the passage, says: " You tell me that you are like me, that you are my *calf*. I am the horned bull: thou wantest the rough head and the horns of the animal, completely to resemble your father." The force of absurdity could go no further unless it went further in the attempted elucidation of another commentator, Henley, who says that Leontes meant to tell the child that to be a calf, he must have a tuft on his forehead, and the young horns that shoot from it ! as if Leontes had a tuft on his forehead, and the horns were not the figurative horns with which the heads of cuckolds were supposed to be burthened !

PENDRAGON.

The dramatists of the Elizabethan era do not seem to have been greatly fascinated by the Keltic legends that refer to the name and exploits of the great King Arthur, although they offered such abundant material for dramatic poetry. Falstaff, in the 2nd Part of *Henry IV.*, Act. IV. Sc. 2, sings a fragment of the old ballad of *Sir Lancelot Du Lake* :—

> When *Arthur* first in court began,
> And was approved king.

The ballad literature of the sixteenth and seventeenth centuries was enriched with the traditions, more or less mythological, that pertained to the name of this greatest favourite of all the Keltic nations, but it remained to a poet of our time to produce a work worthy of so great a memory. But neither in Shakspeare's day nor in our own was there, or is there, any correct notion existent in the popular mind of the meaning of the word *Pendragon*, bestowed upon Arthur himself and on his supposed father Uther. The commonly-received opinion was, and is, that the word was related, in some way or other, to the fabulous monster—so familiar in Heraldry—the *Dragon*. Alfred Tennyson, in the *Idylls of the King*, speaks of King Arthur's golden helmet, on which he bore

> The dragon of the great Pendragonship.

But *Pendragon* is neither a proper name, as some have supposed, nor a crest in the form of a helmet, as Ritson suggests, nor has it any relation to a dragon. It was undoubtedly the real title of a chief warrior among the Keltic nations. When the Romans abandoned Britain, the several petty kings who shared the dominion between them, each independent, or semi-independent of the other, found it necessary to unite for mutual defence against the invading hordes of North Germany that harried and despoiled their coasts, and strove to reduce them to subjection. For this purpose a chief king was chosen, to preside over their councils and direct their operations in war. This great personage was called the *Pen-dragon.* One of the first who bore the title was Vortigern, whose name in Keltic (*Fior-tighearn*) signifies the "true Lord." After him came the father of Arthur, and Arthur himself. Possibly many other and forgotten chieftans bore the same title. The word is derived from the Kymric *Pen*, head, chief; *drag*, a section; and *dragon*, a leader in war. From these words comes *Pendragon*, the leader of all the sections; that is to say, an Emperor. In our day, if the Kymric, or Keltic, was the language in use, Queen Victoria would be called the *Pendragon* of India; and the King of Prussia, the *Pendragon* of the German Empire.

QUAIL AND CALLET.

These words, used contemptuously by Shakspeare, signify a woman of light behaviour or loose morals :—

> Here's Agamemnon,—an honest fellow enough, and one that loves *quails*.
>
> —*Troilus and Cressida*, Act V. Sc. 1.

"The *quail*," says Nares, "was thought to be a very amorous bird; hence the metaphor." In this instance Nares jumped to an erroneous conclusion—to the disadvantage of the *quail*, which is no more amorous than a sparrow or any other bird. Ben Jonson, thinking that *Quail* was only metaphorically used for a woman, employs *plover* in the same sense in *Bartholomew Fair*, Act IV. Sc. 5. Shakspeare makes Leontes, in his wrath, rail at

Paulina, who presents his new-born daughter to him, and
calls her—

> A callat,
> Of boundless tongue, who late hath beat her husband,
> And now baits me !
>
> *Winter's Tale*, Act II. Sc. 3.

And again—

> He called her whore ; a beggar, in his drink,
> Could not have laid such terms upon his *callat.*
>
> —*Othello*, Act IV. Sc. 2.

Quail, Callet, and *Callat* are all derived from the Keltic
caile, a girl, and *cailleach,* an old woman.

SHREW.

Few words in the English language have excited greater
controversy as to its origin than this, and few have been
more largely twisted from their first meaning. A *Shrew* is
a noisy and ill-tempered woman ; a *shrewd* man is a
cunning and sagacious, but may be a very quiet and good-
natured. person ; while to have a " *shrewd* suspicion," is to
have a suspicion that appears in the estimation of its
entertainer to be more then commonly well founded.
Shrew and *shrewd* would thus appear to be related
in sound, but unrelated in meaning. The currently accepted
etymology of *shrew* is from the German *Schreien,* to cry
out in a shrill voice, from whence comes *shrick.*

The derivation from *shrew-mouse,* because that little
animal was supposed to be particularly vicious, has long
been abandoned by philologists, though a few still remain
who cling to it. The Germans translated the English "to
shrew" by *Verfluchen,* to curse—and a *shrew,* by *Zankerinn*
'a female who quarrels), *Keiferinn* (a female who chides or
scolds), and by *Ein böses weib* (a bad or wicked woman)

These all convey the modern English meaning of a *shrew*, but do not in the slightest degree approach the etymology. The French have *Mégère*, from the Greek, a fury, and *Grondeuse*, a woman who grumbles or scolds. The only other possible source of the English word must be sought in the Keltic, where we find *sior* (sheer), perpetual; and *ruag*, to persecute, to annoy, to vex, to harass, to torment; whence *sior ruag* (*sheeruag*), anglicised and abbreviated into *shrew*, a perpetual worry, vexation, or annoyance. The word has also been derived from *sruth* (*sru*), to flow, applied metaphorically to an unceasing flow or flux (of angry words). Neither of these derivations, if either may be accepted— would confine the opprobrious epithet to women, but would apply equally to men, as Shakspeare has it in the *Taming of the Shrew* :—

> By this reckoning, he is more a *shrew* than she.

and in *Gammer Gurton* :—

> Come on, old fellow ! it is told me thou art a *shrew*.

The noun is probably from *sior ruag*. The verb " to *shrew*," to curse, is probably from *sru*, to curse with a *running* or flux, as in the couplet in *Love's Labour Lost* (Act V. Sc. 2) where the word is written *shrows*, and when in allusion to pock-marks, Rosaline says :—

> O that your face were not so full of O's ;

and the Princess replies—

> A pox of that jest ! and I *beshrew* all *shrows*.

SLIGHT.

This is a word of many meanings : *Slight*, is frail or fragile ; to *slight*, is to despise or scorn, or think lightly of a person or thing ; *slight*, is to eject or throw out, as Fal-

staff was *slighted* from the buckbasket into the Thames.
It is used by Shakspeare in the sense of a trick, artifice,
or contrivance, and survives to this time as *slight* or *sleight-
of-hand*, a conjuring trick. The French have translated
this phrase into *leger-de-main*, or light of hand ; and the
English have adopted it again, to express " conjuring ": -

> And that distilled by magic *slights*,
> Shall raise such artificial sprites.
>
>   —*Macbeth*, Act III. Sc. 5.

Nares and others define *slight* where it occurs in *Twelfth
Night* as an abbreviation of " by this light."

> '*Slight*, I could so beat the rogue.
>
>   —Act II. Sc. 5.
>
> '*Slight !* will you make an ass of me ?
>
>   —Act III. Sc. 2.

How wrong these explanations are, and what is the true
source of *slight* or *sleight* of hand, will appear from the Keltic
slaight, a piece of roguery, a deception, a trick ; *slaight*,
slaightear, a rogue, a rascal, a cheat ; and *slaightearachd*,
knavery, conjuration. This accounts for '*slight* in *Macbeth ;*
and '*slight* in *Twelfth Night*, and makes an end of the
derivation which finds favour with Nares, for " by this
light," and converts '*Slight !* will you make an ass of me ? "
into " ' Rogue,' ' cheat,' or ' knave,' will you make an ass of
me ? "

TAKEN WITH THE MANNER.

This appears to have been a proverbial phrase in
Shakspeare's time to signify "taken in the act," or taken
with stolen property still in possession. It occurs in the
first part of *King Henry IV. :—*

> Oh, villain ! thou stolest a cup of sack eighteen years ago, and wert
> *taken with the manner !*
>
>   —Act II. Sc. 4.

It also occurs in *Love's Labour Lost*, where Costard (Act I. Sc. 1) makes several puns upon the word :—

> . . . . The *manner* of it is, I was taken with the *manner*.
>
> *Biron.* In what *manner* ?
>
> *Costard.* In *manner* and *form* following, Sir ; all those three : I was seen with her in the *manor* house, sitting with her upon the *form*, and taken following her into the park ; which, put together, is in *manner* and *form* following. Now, Sir, for the *manner*,—it is the *manner* of a man to speak to a woman : for the *form*,—in some *form*.

In the old Law Books, *mainour*, *manour*, and *meinour* are derived from the French *manier*, to handle or lay hold of, and are said to signify, in a legal sense, the thing taken away, or found in the *hand* of the thief who has stolen it. But this derivation is unsatisfactory. What is called New Latin, including many law terms, is formed of Keltic words with Latin terminations, such, for instance, as "burglary," which is derived from the Keltic *buar*, cattle, *glac*, to seize, whence a *buarglacair*, one who committed a burglary, one of the earliest forms of robbery in a pastoral country. In like manner (no pun intended), *Taken with* or *in the manner* is derived from the Keltic *mainnir*, and *manrach*, a sheep-fold, and signified originally a sheep-stealer, detected in the fold, and in the very act of stealing the animals.

TAWDRY.

This word, as used by Shakspeare and his contemporaries, seems to have signified an ornament for the neck or arm, either of lace or jewellery ; and never to have been employed as a depreciatory epithet—as in the modern sense of gaudy, but worthless, or of small intrinsic value. In

Winter's Tale (Act IV. Sc. 3) the rustic wench Mopsa says to the Clown :—

> You promised me a *tawdry* lace and a pair of sweet gloves.

Here it is evident that Mopsa did not mean anything worthless. In Drayton's *Polyolbion* the poet says :—

> The blue Nereids
> Make *tawdries* for their necks.

The origin of the word has never been correctly traced. All the etymologists have derived it from *Saint Audrey*, or *Etheldreda*, because an annual fair was held on St. Audrey's day, in some town or village in the Isle of Ely, or some part of Lincolnshire, and which became famous for the sale of cheap flimsy ornaments for the adornment of women. Mr. Wedgwood does not admit the accuracy of this derivation, but he suggests no other. Nares, who is contented with the derivation from St. Audrey or St. Etheldreda, narrates that an old historian makes St. Audrey die of a swelling in her throat, which she considered as a particular judgment upon her, for having been in her youth too much addicted to wearing fine necklaces! The credulous historian, and the too easily satisfied philologist, in accepting *necklace* as the original meaning of the word, came very near the truth without knowing it. The word in the Keltic signified, not a necklace, but a *bracelet*, or ornament for the arm, from *taod*, a rope, a string, a lace, a small chain of gold ; and *righe*, the arm ; whence *taod-righe*, corrupted into *Tawdry*. When the original Keltic meaning became obscured, and the sense was finally lost, the word was held to signify any ornament for the person. None of the quotations from Shakspeare and the Elizabethan writers conveys the modern idea that the *tawdries* were necessarily valueless or vulgar.

TEAR CAT.

This odd epithet was applied in the seventeenth century to violent and ranting actors, who overdid their parts—

> *D.* What's thy name, fellow soldier?
>
> *T.* I am called, by those who have seen my valour, *Tear Cat.*
>
> —*Old Play (quoted by Nares).*

> I could play Ercles rarely, or a part to *tear a cat* in.
>
> —*Midsummer Night's Dream*, Act I. Sc. 2.

> I had rather hear two good jests, than a whole play of such *tear cat* thunderbolts.
>
> —Day's *Isle of Gulls.*

Nares suggests that probably the phrase originated from a cruel act of this kind (tearing a cat) having been performed by some daring ruffian to create surprise and alarm. As if in corroboration of this opinion, Mr. Staunton cites from an anonymous author, "Sirrah! this is you that would rend or *tear-a-cat* upon the stage," from *Histriomastix, or the Players Whipt* (1610). It is difficult to believe that such a brutal and disgusting action, taking the words in their literal Saxon sense, could ever have happened, or could have been tolerated on the English stage, and just as difficult not to believe that the words were a corruption of a similarly sounding phrase in the vernacular. Such words are to be found in the Keltic *dur* or *duire*, obstinate, and *cath* (Kymric *càd*), a battle, whence (*d* pronounced as *t*) *duire-cath*, an obstinate or fierce single-handed combat on the stage, between two violent actors, desirous of pleasing the gallery or the groundlings of the pit. The allusion by Bottom the Weaver to the part of Ercles, which, he thought he could "play rarely," lends force to this interpretation.

TROJAN.

When Shakspeare, in *Henry V.*, uses the word *Trojan*, does he mean a thief? which Nares conjectures he does.

Dost thou think, base *Trojan*, to have me fold up Parca's fatal web?

or does he mean, in the Homeric sense of the word, a warrior of Troy?

Mr. Halliwell defines *Trojan* as "a boon companion: a person who is fond of liquor. According to some," he adds, "a thief was so called, but it was applied somewhat indiscriminately." A rough, manly boy is now called a fine *Trojan*. Grose, has "trusty *Trojan*, a true friend."

The word is vernacular English—not Greek, and is derived from the Keltic *troid* (pronounced *troij* or *troidge*), to fight, to contend, to quarrel.

TRUE-PENNY.

Forby, quoted in Halliwell's "Archaic Dictionary," thinks that the application of this phrase by Hamlet to the ghost of his father (Act I. Sc. 5, is unseemly and incongruous, and is of opinion that it means staunch and trusty, true to his purpose or pledge. Mr. Collier, led astray apparently by the word "cellarage" that occurs in the same passage, where the ghost, "from below," exclaims to Horatio and Marcellus, whom Hamlet adjures to secrecy, "Swear!" describes *True-Penny* as a mining term that signifies a particular indication in the soil, of the direction in which ore is to be found. Surely perverted ingenuity never went further! Forby's explanation, derived from the ordinary English sense of *true*, though it takes no account of the word *penny*, is infinitely preferable to Mr. Collier's. It is nevertheless possible that *True-Penny*, apparently used by

Shakspeare in a jocular and disrespectful sense, was intended by the poet to conceal or slur over the deep tragic emotion of Hamlet's mind, so that his two friends might not suspect the intensity of his feeling ; especially as further on in the scene, where the ghost from below again urges them to " swear," he addresses him familiarly as " old mole." Hamlet has, however, addressed the apparition once before with the words, "Alas, poor ghost!" ; and afterwards, in the third reiteration of " swear," adjured it with the words, " Rest, rest, perturbed spirit"; neither of which phrases partakes of irreverence. Perhaps the Keltic etymology of *True-Penny*, as employed in this passage, expresses the real meaning, and conceals a play upon the words identical in sound, but not in meaning, in the Keltic and Saxon. In Keltic *truagh* (pronounced *tru-a*) signifies unhappy, wretched, miserable ; and *peine*, torment or punishment. This, as a phrase of commiseration, should be read by the gloss of the ghost's first speech to Hamlet :—

> I am thy father's spirit :
> Doomed for a certain time to walk the night,
> And for the day condemned to fast in fires ;
> Till the foul crimes, done in my days of nature,
> Are burnt and purged away.

In this sense, *truagh peine* would be a phrase of the deepest pity, and would better suit the solemn character of the whole scene than the ludicrous *True-Penny* in the Saxon sense. *True-Penny* has not been traced to any writer before or contemporary with Shakespeare ; and Johnson's and other dictionaries cite him as the sole authority for it.

WELKIN.

This word, which is usually held to signify the sky, heaven, and what in biblical and non-scientific language was called the " firmament," is derived by all the English dictionaries from the German or Saxon *wealcan*, to roll ; or *welke*, a cloud ; and *wolkenhimmel*, a cloudy sky. Mr. Wedgwood suggests that " perhaps *welke* may be from the German *wolle* (wool , from the woolly aspect of the clouds ": and adds that " the *fleecy* clouds is an habitual metaphor, which is also to be found in Virgil."

Shakspeare uses *Welkin* in a sense which does not imply cloudiness, as in *Midsummer Night's Dream*, Act III. Sc. 2 :—

> The *starry welkin* cover thee anon
> With drooping fog as black as Acheron.

Chaucer has " In all the *welkin* was no cloud "; and Milton writes, " from either end of heaven the *welkin* burns."

From these instances it is evident that *welkin* signified the sky, but not evident that the word was derived from the clouds.

But the singular phrase, " a *welkin* eye," as used by Shakspeare in the *Winter's Tale*, when Leontes addresses his little son Mamillius, whose paternity he doubts, cannot be satisfactorily explained by the Saxon derivation from " the clouds." To get over this preliminary difficulty, all commentators seem to agree that in this sentence *welkin* means *blue as the welkin ;* or that the father, addressing the child, whom he would fain believe to be his own, but dares not on account of his overpowering and increasing jealousy, uses the word *welkin* to signify blue, like the clear sky :—

> Come, Sir page !
> Look on me with thy *welkin* eye, sweet villain !
> Most dear'st, my collop !   *Can thy dam ?*

Here the unextinguished affection of the father for the child is strongly apparent. He wishes to believe in him, calls him his " dearest," his " collop " (that is, his blossom,

Shakspeare in a jocular and disrespectful sense, was intended by the poet to conceal or slur over the deep tragic emotion of Hamlet's mind, so that his two friends might not suspect the intensity of his feeling ; especially as further on in the scene, where the ghost from below again urges them to "swear," he addresses him familiarly as "old mole." Hamlet has, however, addressed the apparition once before with the words, "Alas, poor ghost!" ; and afterwards, in the third reiteration of "swear," adjured it with the words, "Rest, rest, perturbed spirit"; neither of which phrases partakes of irreverence. Perhaps the Keltic etymology of *True-Penny*, as employed in this passage, expresses the real meaning, and conceals a play upon the words identical in sound, but not in meaning, in the Keltic and Saxon. In Keltic *truagh* (pronounced *tru-a*) signifies unhappy, wretched, miserable ; and *peine*, torment or punishment. This, as a phrase of commiseration, should be read by the gloss of the ghost's first speech to Hamlet :—

> I am thy father's spirit :
> Doomed for a certain time to walk the night,
> And for the day condemned to fast in fires ;
> Till the foul crimes, done in my days of nature,
> Are burnt and purged away.

In this sense, *truagh peine* would be a phrase of the deepest pity, and would better suit the solemn character of the whole scene than the ludicrous *True-Penny* in the Saxon sense. *True-Penny* has not been traced to any writer before or contemporary with Shakespeare ; and Johnson's and other dictionaries cite him as the sole authority for it.

WELKIN.

This word, which is usually held to signify the sky, heaven, and what in biblical and non-scientific language was called the "firmament," is derived by all the English dictionaries from the German or Saxon *wealcan*, to roll ; or *wolke*, a cloud ; and *wolkenhimmel*, a cloudy sky. Mr. Wedgwood suggests that " perhaps *wolke* may be from the German *wolle* (wool , from the woolly aspect of the clouds"; and adds that " the *fleecy* clouds is an habitual metaphor, which is also to be found in Virgil."

Shakspeare uses *Welkin* in a sense which does not imply cloudiness, as in *Midsummer Night's Dream*, Act III. Sc. 2 :—

> The *starry welkin* cover thee anon
> With drooping fog as black as Acheron.

Chaucer has " In all the *welkin* was no cloud "; and Milton writes, " from either end of heaven the *welkin* burns."

From these instances it is evident that *welkin* signified the sky, but not evident that the word was derived from the clouds.

But the singular phrase, " a *welkin* eye," as used by Shakspeare in the *Winter's Tale*, when Leontes addresses his little son Mamillius, whose paternity he doubts, cannot be satisfactorily explained by the Saxon derivation from " the clouds." To get over this preliminary difficulty, all commentators seem to agree that in this sentence *welkin* means *blue as the welkin ;* or that the father, addressing the child, whom he would fain believe to be his own, but dares not on account of his overpowering and increasing jealousy, uses the word *welkin* to signify blue, like the clear sky :—

> Come, Sir page !
> Look on me with thy *welkin* eye, sweet villain !
> Most dear'st, my collop !   *Can thy dam ?*

Here the unextinguished affection of the father for the child is strongly apparent. He wishes to believe in him, calls him his " dearest," his " collop " (that is, his blossom,

bud or sprout—*see* that word), and asks him to look at him
with his *welkin eye*, and then asks again, "Can thy dam?"
—*i.e.,* "Can thy mother look at me with a *welkin eye* as
thou canst?" If *welkin* means blue as the sky, it would
follow that both the child and the mother had blue eyes:
and that if one could look at him with such an eye, so
could the other. But Leontes doubted the mother in spite
of her blue eyes—if they *were* blue, and not grey or black,
as they might have been for all that appears in the play.
If *clear* as the sky, and not *blue* as the sky, be accepted as
the true meaning of Shakspeare's epithet, the Saxon etymology from *wolken* (or the clouds) would have to be rejected.
Possibly the true origin of the word in this sense may be
the Keltic *uile*, all; and *cean* (kean), love, favour, fondness,
kindness; whence *uile-cean*, the all-loving, the all-fond eye
of the innocent child. Interpreted by this gloss, the passage would be: Look at me with thy clear, certain, endear-
ing, and *all-loving* eye. Can thy dam, or mother, do as
much?

In the child's clear, innocent, and loving eye he refused
to see uncertainty or falsehood, and implicitly relied on its
truth and ingenuousness. In the mother's eye he had no
such confidence, and hence the question—"Can thy dam?"

This suggestion is offered, undogmatically and simply, as
one that merits consideration from all who would, if possible, extract light from the darker passages of a poet who
always thought clearly and expressed himself plainly, and
all whose seeming obscurities are due either to the printer
or to our own ignorance of the colloquial language of his
time and his native Warwickshire. Another beautiful idea
would spring from the word *welkin* if *uile-cean* could be
accepted as the true etymology—namely, that the *welkin*
was the *all-loving* heavens, and so addressed and so considered by the earliest nations in the dawn of their religion
and poetry. Whatever hatred there might be on the earth,
heaven was all-loving.

"Sky," in English, did not originally signify heaven—the clear expanse without cloud—but cloud itself, or an excrescence upon the blue purity of the "firmament." Chaucer says :—

> A certain winde
> That blew so hideously and hie,
> That it ne lefte not a *skie*
> In all the *welkin* long and brode.
>
> —*House of Fame*, Book III.

And Gower also :—

> All so deirly
> She passeth as it were a *skie*.
> All clere out of this ladies' sight.
>
> —*Confessio Amantis*.

From these and other passages that might be cited from the pre-Shakspearean poets, it is evident that *welkin* and *sky* were not synonymous, as they afterwards became ; that the word *welkin* had no reference to clouds ; and that the phrase a "cloudy sky" was pleonastic.